Discard

Great Careers for People Interested in
Math & Computers

by
Peter Richardson
and
Bob Richardson

An Imprint of Gale Research Inc.

Library of Congress Catalog Card Number 93-78079
ISBN 0-8103-9385-9

Acknowledgments
The authors and the publishers wish
to thank those people whose careers
are featured in this book for allowing
us to interview and photograph them
at work. Their love for their chosen
careers has made our task an
enjoyable one. We also thank Paul
Winter and Patrick J. Winter for
supplying samples of programs and
machine code and for sharing their
experiences of mathematical puzzles,
computer games, and games in
general. Thanks go as well to all
those who assisted us with the
photography: Jessica Deutsch-Goulet;
Karin Kozen and John Kozen (Matrix
Design Consultants); Barb Zoltok
(Mastermind Educational); and Oma
Sewhdat (IBM); Andrea Chamczuk,
the Rose family, the O'Hara family,
the Cascone family, and the Winter
family, for agreeing to appear in this
volume.

Design concept: Julian Cleva
Design and layout: Warren Clark
Editors: Mary Kay Winter, Jane McNulty
Proofreaders: Diane Klim, Anna Marie Salvia

Printed and bound in Canada
10 9 8 7 6 5 4 3 2 1

This book's text stock contains more
than 50% recycled paper.

Contents

Hazel de Burgh

Forensic Accountant

PERSONAL PROFILE

Career: Forensic accountant. "I've always been interested in law and accounting. I've got the best of both worlds!"

Interests: Sailing, skiing, scuba diving, windsurfing, camping, and canoeing.

Latest accomplishment: Testifying in court. Her evidence was accepted by the judge and helped him make his decision.

Why I do what I do: "Working on cases is like solving puzzles. Each case is a new challenge and I'm energized by challenges."

I am: Thorough, determined, and assertive. "It's exciting when we start getting some answers and are close to solving a case."

What I wanted to be when I was in school: "I thought about being a doctor or a lawyer. Then I considered being an airline pilot. I finally decided I wanted to do something in math."

What a forensic accountant does

Accountants are trained to understand and maintain financial records. They usually work for individuals or businesses, helping them to keep track of their finances. They also give advice about money management. Records of financial deals allow you to keep track of how much you've earned and how much you've spent. And if someone else, such as the government, wants to check your finances, you need accurate records to show what you have done.

But accounting can involve a lot more than just keeping track of other people's money. It can also involve investigating missing money, such as when employees steal from their company. When that happens, a unique kind of accountant is needed to help solve the puzzle. Hazel de Burgh is such a person. She's a forensic and investigative accountant. That's like having an accountant, a lawyer, and a detective rolled into one. "Like all accountants, I know how to interpret financial statements and other accounting records," says Hazel. "But I'm trained as well to investigate theft, fraud, and financial deals. I also use my knowledge of legal matters to help lawyers resolve lawsuits."

The dictionary defines "forensic" as something "used in a court of law." A forensic accountant follows accounting procedures to gather evidence that could be used in court or in out-of-court proceedings.

"Each case I work on offers something new," says Hazel. "Cases can be short or long, simple or complex. The police, for example, might hire us to help with a criminal investigation where they think a large amount of money has disappeared.

A forensic accountant's job is many-sided. As well as juggling numbers on a computer, Hazel works like a master sleuth, following the trail of evidence wherever it may lead.

Or a company might want us to investigate an employee suspected of stealing. Sometimes one company might ask us to help them decide whether or not it's a good business deal to buy another company. We're experts at assessing the accuracy of financial information, finding evidence, and helping to catch financial crooks."

Big companies have so much money that some people feel tempted to steal from them. They don't think they'll get caught — they think the money won't be missed or can't be traced to them. If a lot of money disappears from a business's accounts, a forensic accountant may be called in to determine how much is missing, who took it, and where it went.

White-collar crime

When most people think of crime, they think of murder, assault, bank robberies, or auto theft. But there is another type of crime that is even more difficult to prevent. "White-collar crime" refers to illegal financial transactions, such as embezzlement of funds, fraud, or financial swindles. Crimes like these may be committed by people with very responsible high-level jobs. They carry out their crimes while at work, using the computers and financial systems of their companies.

How serious a problem is white-collar crime? It's estimated that each year four or five times as much money is lost because of white-collar crime compared to all other types of crime combined.

All in a day's work

"I work on many cases at the same time," says Hazel. She often travels to different cities and meets many interesting people. "The deadlines vary. Complicated cases may take more than a year, while others are resolved more quickly." According to Hazel, once you understand the problem in a company, there are five stages to every case:

"First, we need to figure out a strategy. This is one of the most exciting stages. We assess all the issues and determine how to resolve each one. At this stage, we may meet with the client to make sure that everyone understands and agrees to the approach.

"Then we have to gather the evidence. This involves thinking about what evidence we'll need. Evidence might include financial statements, diaries and date books, invoices and other accounting records describing sales and purchases, and minutes of company meetings. We may have to interview people who work at the company or outside the company. This often provides valuable information and can help to identify the truth.

"Analyzing the evidence is the third step. Often we work as a team to examine the documentary evidence and the testimony of the people interviewed. It's like solving a puzzle. We get as many pieces as we can to fit together. This gives us a good idea of what has happened. It's great when it all starts coming together at this stage.

"Reporting our conclusions is the fourth step. We give a report to the people who need to know our findings. These people can include

lawyers, company management, or the police.

"And finally," says Hazel, "for about 5 percent of our cases, we may have to present the evidence in court. Presenting in court involves testifying as an expert witness." (An expert witness can give opinions on a court case. A regular witness can only report the facts.) "I report the facts and provide my opinion about what it all means. This is the ultimate challenge and excitement. It's not for everyone, though. I have to be tough and be able to take the heat of cross-examination."

Suing for loss of profits

Hazel has worked on many different cases. One involved a lawsuit between two companies we'll call ABC and XYZ. According to ABC, XYZ was supposed to supply ABC with special parts needed to build its machines. But XYZ failed to supply enough parts; as a result, ABC's production slowed down. ABC made fewer machines and, of course, fewer sales. It blamed its losses on XYZ's failure to supply as many parts as promised. ABC hired Hazel's company to determine how much ABC lost because of XYZ's actions.

"We had to find evidence to prove how many more machines ABC could have sold if XYZ had fulfilled its agreement. Our analysis of these

records helped us conclude how much profit ABC had lost. The judge accepted my opinion and ordered XYZ to pay ABC the amount that I had calculated."

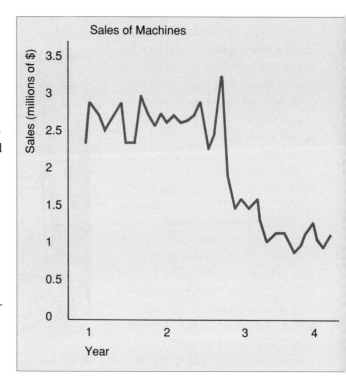

Hazel explains, "If a graph shows a steady rate of sales and then suddenly falls, showing a loss of sales, we wonder why. What happened during this period of time that would explain the loss of sales? What do these numbers tell us?"

Too many bills

Hazel worked on another case in which a lawyer was accused of overbilling. He had worked for the government's legal aid plan, which provides lawyers for people who need representation in court but who can't afford to pay the lawyer's fee. This lawyer had worked for several clients over a period of months. Hazel's company was hired to figure out how much he had overbilled.

"The lawyer had separate invoices for each client. We fed this information into a database in a computer. The computer arranged the invoices in chronological order so we could see, day by day, the hours he claimed for all his clients. We found that on many days he had billed for more work than he could possibly have done. On some days his invoices told us he had worked more than 24 hours! We also found that he had billed for work he couldn't have done because he was in court on that day. By using the computer to sort out his invoices, we got a clearer picture of how he was cheating the legal aid plan."

Psychology of interviews

Hazel's job involves more than analyzing financial documents. "When I'm interviewing someone involved in a case, I have to be aware of how the person is reacting to my questions," explains Hazel. "I like reading books on human behavior and psychology. They give me insight into how people react." Most people are nervous during interviews. It's natural to feel this way. But Hazel needs to be aware of any abnormal behavior during an interview. "We have to figure out if someone is lying to us. If a person appears too nervous or too confident, that might suggest a cover-up. If I ask a difficult question, does the person clam up or become evasive? These are just a few of the many questions we have to keep in mind during an interview. I rely on my intuition and my knowledge of human behavior to tell me if something is wrong." If Hazel thinks someone is lying, she asks herself, "What is this person hiding? How does this affect the case?"

Activity

Fraud artist at work

Jo's Milk Mart is open 24 hours. There are three shifts — the day shift (8:00 a.m. to 4:00 p.m.), the evening shift (4:00 p.m. to midnight) and the night shift (midnight to 8:00 a.m.). At the end of each shift, the manager bundles up the cash and takes it to the bank. The graph shows the three daily deposits over three weeks. The table shows who was the manager on each shift. Jo begins to suspect that one of the managers is pocketing some of the money.

Week	Managers		
	Day	Evening	Night
1	Jose	Leslie	Maria
2	Maria	Jose	Leslie
3	Leslie	Maria	Jose

1. From the graph, what evidence is there to make Jo suspect fraud?
2. From the information in the graph and the table, whom would you finger as the suspect?
3. Suppose weather records show that it rained every night in Week 2. How would this affect the case against your suspect?
4. Suppose this kind of data is the only evidence available. Do you think this is enough to get a conviction in court? How many weeks' evidence do you think would be enough?
5. What else, besides the weather, do you think might affect the amount of sales on any day or in any week?

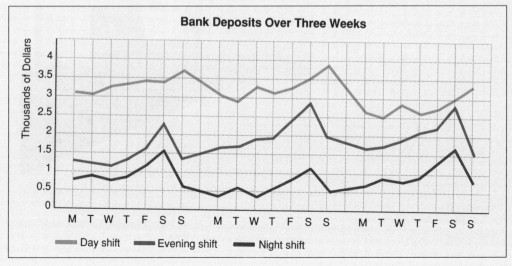

Bank Deposits Over Three Weeks

Day shift — Evening shift — Night shift

How to become a forensic accountant

In high school, Hazel took a lot of math and science courses. "I was always good in math," she says. "I took English and French, too. Communication skills are very important in my work. I also found typing very helpful.

We didn't have computers in high school then, but later I used them a lot."

Hazel enrolled in a four-year co-op program at a university. During that time, she alternated between four-month school terms and four-month work terms. "I really liked this program. I learned math, computers, and accounting in the classroom and had practical training on the job. It was a great way to learn."

After receiving her degree, Hazel studied for exams to become a chartered accountant. When she passed the final exam and completed a year of articling, she was officially a C.A. (A C.A., or Chartered Accountant in Canada, is the equivalent of a C.P.A., or Certified Public Accountant, in the United States.) After that she was contracted to the police as their in-house accountant. "They needed someone with accounting knowledge to help them solve cases. I worked with the police for a year. That experience was the start of my career as a forensic accountant."

Is this career for you?

For this career, you need determination. "Sometimes you can get stalled," says Hazel, "but it's important to keep at it. You have to get over any hurdles and follow a case through until you solve it." You need good communication skills. You will find yourself working with many professional people, such as lawyers and police officers. It's important to be able to make yourself understood.

Being thorough is very important. You can't rush through a case because your conclusions might turn out to be wrong. "Sometimes the information you get doesn't make a lot of sense. It takes a lot of work to get to the bottom of a problem and figure out what's going on. I enjoy dealing with clients personally, and helping them with their problems. After reporting our findings, it feels good to know we've done a thorough job."

Much as Hazel loves her job, she does admit that she sometimes has too much on the go at once. "I might be working on 10 to 20 cases at the same time. Sometimes it can be tough meeting all my deadlines."

Hazel's company rents offices high above the city. Their clients — lawyers, large corporations, and police departments — are likely to be centrally located in large population centers.

Career planning

In the phone book, find the name of a business college that offers courses in bookkeeping and accounting. Phone the college and ask for information about courses.

Making Career Connections

Invite a police officer or a forensic accountant to your school to speak about white-collar crime. Take notes on the presentation.

Write to a professional accountants' association. Ask about other fields in which accountants might specialize.

In a computer store, ask about programs that are used by bookkeepers and accountants. Find out how much computer equipment you would need to set yourself up as a freelance bookkeeper.

Getting started

Interested in being a forensic accountant? Here's what you can do now.

1. Take math and English courses in school.
2. Join a debating club and take part in debates. Debating will help you learn how to formulate an argument and improve your speaking skills.
3. Stand up and speak to a group of people whenever you get the chance.
4. Read newspaper stories involving legal cases and business crimes.

Related careers

Here are some related careers you may want to check out.

Accountant
Maintains or inspects financial records for individuals or businesses, and helps them manage their money.

Bookkeeper
Maintains financial records according to rules established by accountants. May be employed in a company or may do freelance work for several companies. Increasingly, a bookkeeper's work is done on a computer.

Auditor
An accountant who checks financial records to see that they are accurate.

Your local police department may have a specialist in white-collar crime who could tell you more about forensic accounting.

Future watch

Forensic accounting is a new field. More and more accounting firms now have a forensic department to investigate white-collar crime and resolve legal problems. A few companies, like Hazel's firm, focus entirely on forensic accounting. As long as there are lawsuits or white-collar crime, there will be a need for forensic accountants. Because of their familiarity with the law and the legal system, they are well-placed to solve these financial puzzles.

Audio Engineer

PERSONAL PROFILE

Career: Audio engineer. "I've always been fascinated by sound. In school, I was involved with theater productions and the school band."

Interests: Music, swimming, going out with friends, reading trade magazines. "I love movies, too. I like to analyze a sound track and think about how the different sounds were made."

Latest accomplishment: Working as a dialogue editor on the sound effects for a television movie about vampires.

Why I do what I do: "I love working with audio; it's a very creative industry. I never do the same thing twice."

I am: Curious, patient, friendly, and creative.

What I wanted to be when I was in school: "First, I wanted to be a pilot. Then in high school I got involved with a band and decided I wanted to get into the recording industry."

What an audio engineer does

In the world of movies, sound is an important part of the product. If the dialogue in a movie is hard to hear, or if the music is too loud, or if the sounds don't match up with the pictures on the screen, the movie won't be a success. People won't enjoy watching it. "An audio engineer helps an artist with the sound recording," says Rob Hegedus. "We control the sound, to make it as good as it can be. It's a complicated job."

Rob spends most of his time working on shows for television. But audio engineers can work on a wide range of material. The work includes TV and radio commercials, movies, music, and corporate videos. Even the recording of a single song can be a challenge. If the sounds are badly mixed, the volume of the drums could be too loud. You might not be able to hear the other instruments. The talent of the artist might not be fairly represented.

"Corporate videos are high-tech sales pitches," says Rob. "Companies produce them as advertising for potential investors. For example, a company may want to sell shares in a new resort hotel. They'll prepare a video showing the beautiful scenery in the area, along with narration that describes the features of the resort. We'll have to find suitable pre-recorded music to accompany the pictures."

Rob's company usually works on videos that are completed except for the sound. That is, they work on "post-audio" production. Rob might have to record the narration or "edit out" unwanted sounds on the sound track. "Using our equipment, we can edit dialogue, add sound effects and music, and clean up the sound track so it fits the pictures."

Computers and sound

In the past, all the sounds were recorded on tapes. Editing was time-consuming. To remove or to add anything, the editor had to cut the tapes and then splice them back together. Now the computer has revolutionized the recording industry, allowing a single individual to accomplish much more.

"Computers also give us more creative freedom," says Rob. "We can record up to 48 different sounds at once. These sounds are then transferred to the computer's memory. The complete sequence of sounds is stored in the computer. We can go back later and make changes to a certain sound. For example, we might increase the volume of a scream to make a scene more dramatic.

"In the past, everything was recorded on tapes. If your original tapes were destroyed, you'd lose everything. With a computer, there's much less chance of that happening."

In the old days, sounds were recorded on different tracks and had to be mixed by hand. Putting them together to make a song required five or six people sitting at a console, working together. When the system is computerized, only one person is needed to operate the console.

Sound biz terms

Sound track: All the sound in a film or TV show.

Dubbing: Adding sound to an existing sound track, for example, dubbing English into the sound track of a French film.

Post-audio production: The work on a sound track that's done after a film or TV show has been edited.

Mixing: Putting sounds together to produce a sound track.

Rough edit: A show in which all the scenes are in order, but the sound track still needs work.

Fader: A device in a recording console that increases or decreases the signal, increasing or decreasing the volume.

Final cut: Final version of a film.

Track: The part of a tape where a single channel of information is recorded.

All in a day's work

On any day, Rob might work on a television movie, then do a commercial for radio. Or he might have several jobs in a day. He explains, "I do a lot of editing of dialogue for TV shows and commercials. Our clients have their own ideas about what sound they want. It's my job to give the clients what they want in a creative way."

Sound and vision

The first step in TV post-audio production is a screening of the rough edit. This is usually held at the TV studio where the show was made. "Our audio engineers and editors sit down with the producers and the director, who tell us what they want changed or added to the sound track. Basically, they say, 'Here's the job and here are the guidelines. Go to it.' Then it's left in our hands. If we're unsure about something later, such as a bit of dialogue that doesn't sound right, we can meet again and ask them what they want."

Before Rob starts working, he has to make sure the computer is all set. Computers are great tools, but they have to be cared for. "First thing in the morning, I'll set up the system and get it ready for the day's work," says Rob. This involves loading the software — the programs that allow you to edit the sound. There are many programs available for the different computers on the market. Rob uses the most advanced software available for the computers at his studio. "I'll also run anti-virus programs. Computer viruses are a real threat and we've got to guard the system against them." (See "Virus!" on page 25.)

Sound in a TV program

Once the computer is ready, Rob and his fellow engineers start to work on a TV program. "To do the post-audio, we need the final cut of the TV show. This comes from the video editing house." A video editing house concentrates on the visual side of a project. They put all the scenes together in the proper order. When they hand over the job to Rob's company, everything except the sound track is completed. There may be sound in the unfinished show, but it needs to be cleaned up. Lines of dialogue might need re-recording or there might be unwanted sounds that have to be removed. "Along with the final on-air version of the show, we get a computer disk that contains a list of changes to be made in the sound track. Each change has a code number that tells the computer where it can be found on the unedited sound track and where it should be placed in the final cut."

Foley artist

Computers are an important part of the recording industry today. But what if none of the sounds on the computer is right for a particular scene? Enter the foley artist. Foley artists work in the studio, creating live sounds to match the images on the screen. For example, if the audio engineers need the sound of someone walking, a foley artist will walk around the studio, mimicking the movements of the actor in the film. For the sound of someone being punched, the foley artist will punch a sandbag or a piece of beef. If someone is falling down a set of stairs in the film, the foley artist might set up microphones in a stairwell and then throw a side of beef down the stairs. To get the sound of bones being broken, chicken bones will be snapped. There's a host of ways to make the sound you want. "And it's fun to watch the foley artist," says Rob.

A foley artist in action, matching his movements to the image on the screen.

"Suppose we're looking for the sound of a cat's meow," says Rob. "I just type 'cat's meow' into the computer and the computer calls up 30 to 40 different versions of a cat meowing. We listen to them and choose one that suits the sound track."

Movies and TV shows are not shot in sequence. The first scene of a movie may have been the last scene filmed. The same is true of the sound track. The dialogue and other sounds will be out of sequence. Rob puts all the sounds in the proper order so they fit the edited pictures. "We assemble the bits of sound like assembling the pieces in a big jigsaw puzzle," says Rob. "The computer software makes this pretty easy."

Improving the sound

Sometimes the quality of the sound is not good enough. There may be unwanted sounds in the background, words that are cut short, dialogue that runs too long, or unclear sounds. "We go in and clean up the dialogue," says Rob, "and take out things that shouldn't be there. We can also take an unclear sound and clean it up so it is easier to hear. If a line of dialogue is cut short, we need to get the actor into the studio to re-record it. Using the computer, we can then take the new recording and put it on the sound track exactly where it should be." By

pressing a couple of keys, Rob can get the scene he wants on a TV screen and then match it up with the appropriate sounds in the computer's memory.

Choosing sound effects to add to a sound track is the most creative part of Rob's work. He has to find an appropriate sound from the computer's library. "We have a whole library of sounds on a jukebox with about 240 compact disks. We use the computer to search for the sound we want. I really enjoy this part because we're making a creative contribution to the project.

"Audio engineers are the last to work on a project before it's completed, so we're usually given the least amount of time. We have to work pretty fast; luckily, we have the computer to help us."

Rob in the lobby of his studio, on his way to a private screening of a completed film.

Activity

Be a sound engineer

Listening

When you watch a TV program or a movie, pay attention to the sounds you hear. Can you tell if any dialogue has been dubbed? Can you identify any special sound effects that were probably created in a studio like Rob's? Are there any sounds that occur off screen? Make a list of the sounds and put a check beside the ones you think were added in a studio. Get a friend to do the same, then compare your ideas.

Mixing

Try mixing sounds the old-fashioned way, using tapes. You will need two or three tape recorders. First, make a recording of some simple sounds, such as a drum beat. Then, as you play that sound back, add more sounds and record them on another tape recorder. See what effects you can produce by adjusting the volumes.

How to become an audio engineer

When he was in high school, Rob studied music and got involved with the school band. "I enjoyed working with both audio and video technology in high school. I took an A.V. (audio-visual) course and really enjoyed it. It was evident to me that I would like a career that involved sound recording or video work."

During high school, Rob went on a field trip to a recording studio. "Elton John had recorded at this studio; it was interesting. It made me more aware of technology, although at the time no one was using computers."

After high school, Rob went to college where he learned a number of different skills, including sound recording, photography, and video production. After graduation, he worked for a while as a landscaper. "It had nothing to do with sound, but I had to pay the bills," he laughs. "One of the people I worked with had a contact that helped me land my present job. I guess this proves that it helps to know a lot of people and to talk with them about what you're interested in.

"My first job in the sound studio was hard labor, moving equipment," says Rob. "But at the same time, I got a lot of on-the-job training. The experienced audio engineers taught me a lot about recording techniques. I worked my way up, and I'm now an audio engineer myself."

In the good old days...

In the early days of talkies, there was limited technology for making sound tracks. In a lot of old films, the dialogue might be muffled or the music might be very loud and harsh. But considering the equipment available, sound engineers did a pretty good job.

Sound engineers had to use imagination to get special effects. If a director wanted a sound to fade out, the sound technician would actually take a piece of sandpaper and scrape it along the sound track on the film itself. This practice was time-consuming and destructive. Today, audio engineers can pick and choose sounds they want on the sound track. Special effects can be produced by hitting a few keys on a computer.

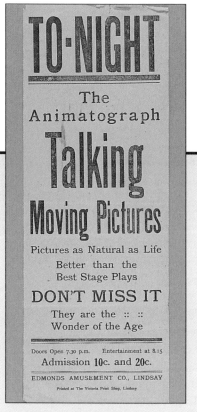

The earliest movies were silent. In theaters, pianists played "live" music to accompany the action on the screen. When sound tracks were included in later movies, the movies were called "talkies."

Is this career for you?

"The minute you start thinking of your job as just something that pays the bills, you lose your creativity. You won't enjoy the work," says Rob. "I like my job so much because I'm interested in all kinds of audio. That's a big reason behind my career choice."

The job involves teamwork among co-workers. "There's a real sense of friendship. Everyone I work with has a great sense of humor. I think you have to be able to laugh at yourself when you make a mistake. You're only human, and so is everyone else. There's no point in getting impatient and frustrated. That just slows you down."

Computers are vital for audio engineers. Rob finds that the technology doesn't hinder creativity; it just gives him more options. "I learned most of my computer skills on the job," says Rob. "But it's a good idea to use computers whenever you can. If you want a job as an audio engineer, you'll have to be computer-literate."

Rob says there's not much he dislikes about his job, but he does occasionally get frustrated with the software for the computers. "If we find a problem in the software, we'll call the software manufacturer and recommend changes that would improve it. If they can't make changes, we have to make do with what we've got.

"Once the final mix is done and the film is ready for viewing, we'll get together with the producers for our own private screening. There's a party atmosphere, and a real sense of accomplishment."

Career planning

Contact one of your local radio stations. Ask permission to visit a studio. If possible, do a "job shadow" as someone is working during a broadcast, and take notes about what the person does.

Making Career Connections

Interview a person who has recorded music in a commercial recording studio. Ask about the experience and take notes or tape record the interview.

Find the name and address of a recording company. Write to the company, asking about jobs in the sound business.

Do you have questions about computers and sound? Find the address of a software company that makes sound cards for personal computers and ask your questions in a letter.

Getting started

Interested in being an audio engineer? Here's what you can do now.

1. Volunteer to help with the sound system at your school assemblies or at a local dance.
2. Learn about computers. Take computer courses, read computer magazines, and get to know about their many uses.
3. Take courses in music if you can. Musical training is not essential, but it can give you an advantage.
4. When you go to a movie or watch a video, think about the sounds you hear; imagine how they could have been made.
5. Plan on studying physics in high school, to learn how sound is produced and how it carries.
6. Read books that describe recording studios and the basics of sound engineering. They should tell you how the best recordings are made.

Related careers

Here are some related careers you may want to check out.

Location recordist
Works with film or TV crews on location. Records dialogue and sound effects.

Software developer for the audio industry
Develops new computer programs that help audio engineers improve the quality and efficiency of their work. Also writes programs for home computers, to help people learn music.

Acoustic engineer
Designs sound recording equipment such as microphones and synthesizers. Also designs sound reproduction equipment such as speakers and compact disk players.

Future watch

This is the information age. Sound plays a key role in transmitting information. There will be a need for creative, computer-literate people in the recording industry.
Audio technology will continue to develop. It will speed up the process of sound track recording and make an audio engineer's job easier and more creative. New technologies will allow people to do high-quality recording at home. In the future, top-notch recordings may be produced in high-tech home studios.

Trevor Brown

Mathematics Consultant

PERSONAL PROFILE

Career: Mathematics consultant. "I'm more interested in math education than math itself. My goal is to find new and better ways to teach math."

Interests: Baseball, hiking, canoeing, skiing. "I also like reading books about math and science."

Latest accomplishment: Writing two math textbooks for grades 7 and 8. Also worked on a math program for a public television station.

Why I do what I do: "My job allows me to work with many different people. Together we try to create new ways of teaching math to students of all ages. I find this exhilarating."

I am: Analytical, systematic, and inquisitive.

What I wanted to be when I was in school: "A teacher. I had some very good teachers and they inspired me and triggered my curiosity."

What a math consultant does

If you don't understand math, how will you pay the bills, do your taxes, or figure out how much to tip at a restaurant? Just about any career requires some problem-solving skills. Architects, plumbers, lawyers, welders, electricians, graphic designers, and physicians all need mathematics to do their jobs properly. Math and computers are for everyone, not just accountants and computer programmers.

Trevor Brown's job is to help math teachers discover ways to make math easier and more exciting for their students. He is a mathematics consultant, working for a school board in a large city. Trevor helps math teachers at 14 schools. "Math involves problem solving and logical thinking," he explains. "We want students to apply math to their own problems as well as to solve the problems in their math books! When they do this, they learn more. We want teachers and students to become actively involved in mathematics. Computers can help with this."

Basically a math consultant's job is to find new and better ways of teaching math and then to help teachers make these changes. Trevor also works with students, parents, and members of the school board. "I'm on call around the clock for our board's math teachers." Trevor stresses the need for discussion. Everyone's input is needed in order to discover the best teaching methods.

Students can become interested and excited about math. Teachers sometimes need to seek out new teaching methods to accomplish this.

"We also keep teachers up-to-date on the latest developments in math. This means reading and going to conferences a lot. We want to know how math is taught in other countries so we can tell our teachers about any new ideas we come across."

Trevor says the most important part of his job is helping students learn that they can do math. Confidence is a key part of learning. "We want kids to feel a sense of their own power to learn. If they have a positive attitude toward math, students can learn what they need to know."

You can do it!

Most of us learn to add and subtract by looking at objects. If we have three balls in front of us and add five more, we can simply count them all. Counting is easy. But when children first learn math symbols, they may have trouble working out an answer. The balls they can see and count are replaced with symbols:

Now they don't have eight objects to count up. This leap from concrete to symbolic math can be tough. Teachers have many "tricks" to help children make the connection. In many different activities, both symbols and real objects are used. Gradually, all the children in a class learn to manipulate the symbols.

$$3 + 5 = ?$$

All in a day's work

Trevor Brown spends most of a day working with people. "On an average morning, I might work with two or three teachers. We'll look at their math program, what they are teaching, and how they are teaching it. Then we sit down and talk. We brainstorm and try to come up with better ways of teaching." But Trevor does not tell the teachers what to do. Teachers must be convinced of the value of any changes before they are used in the classroom. "Discussion is important," says Trevor. "I have to get the trust of teachers. This takes time. Teachers need to feel involved with these new ideas. They need to make the ideas their own."

Evaluating tests

Recently, Trevor had to consider the value of multiple choice tests in which students choose the correct answer from a list. "How should teachers evaluate students? Are teachers giving multiple choice tests mainly because they are easy to mark?" These are two questions Trevor asked himself. "We want to see the steps a student takes to find an answer. We want to assess their understanding. With multiple choice, all a teacher sees is the answer. How

In workshops, parents learn about the math that their children are doing at school.

do we know how the student worked it out?" Trevor feels that some students can get good marks on some multiple choice tests without understanding how they got the answers. With other types of tests, students have to show their work on paper. Trevor comments, "It's important to understand the process involved in getting the answer."

Educating parents

Trevor believes that parents need to know more about how and why math is taught. So he spends a lot of time holding math education workshops for parents. "I often do workshops in the afternoon or after school. These workshops last for about an hour and a half. They deal with math topics, such as geometry, measurement, graphing, and the use of calculators. Workshops let parents know what math is all about, why it is important, and what their children should be learning in school."

Setting guidelines

Trevor and his colleagues at the school board have weekly meetings. They discuss all the latest issues. "We might talk about how the board of education has changed what should be taught in a particular grade." Through these department meetings, Trevor and other consultants will set guidelines for the schools. These guidelines tell teachers what math students should know by a certain age. "We do suggest teaching strategies. Teachers don't have to do exactly what we suggest. But they do have to follow the basic guidelines."

Puzzles

There is more to mathematics than juggling numbers! Creative thinking is needed as well. Try to solve these two puzzles. (Answers are on page 48.)

■ Collect 10 small objects, such as pop bottle tops. Figure out how you can arrange them in four straight rows, with four objects in each row.

■ On a piece of paper, make a square with nine dots, as shown below. Without lifting your pencil from the paper, draw four straight lines that cross all the dots.

Keeping up-to-date

Trevor's work takes him to math conferences around the world. "We have a conference budget," says Trevor. "One or two representatives from our department attend the major conferences. There might be two or three of these conferences in a year,

so we spend some time traveling. It's important that we keep up-to-date on the latest developments in mathematics." Reading is also an essential part of the job. "I get four or five mathematics journals each month. I'm always on the lookout for better ways to teach math in schools."

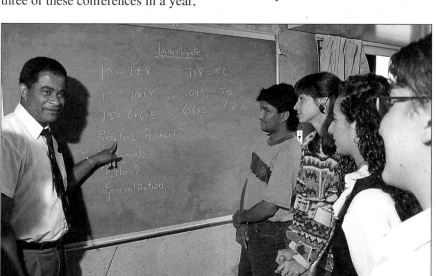

Mathematics, weather forecasting, and megaflops

How far ahead of time can you predict the weather? An hour? A day? A week? The Cray X-MP supercomputer in England uses mathematics to make predictions a week and a half in advance. For this, it is fed data and it does a lot of arithmetic. It calculates at a rate of 800 megaflops. (A megaflop is 1 million arithmetical calculations per second.)

Trevor helps teachers develop a variety of teaching methods. Some students enjoy abstract problems, such as calculating square roots. Others are more interested in practical problems, such as how many hours they'll need to work to save enough money for a new bike.

Activity

Polygons and polyhedrons

You will need
paper
pencil
compass
ruler

A regular polygon is a two-dimensional shape with straight sides that are all the same length. For example, an equilateral triangle is a regular polygon with three sides all the same length. A square is a polygon with four sides the same length. A pentagon has five sides, a

hexagon six, a heptagon seven, and an octagon eight. Try to draw all of these polygons. (Hint: For all of them, start by drawing a circle. Then draw the polygon inside the circle.)

You will need
drinking straws
scissors
thread

The three-dimensional shapes shown here are regular polyhedrons. Their sides are all regular polygons. Cut pieces of drinking straws, put thread through the pieces, and try to make these two regular polyhedrons.

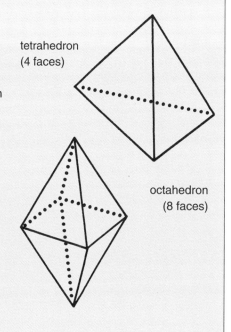

tetrahedron (4 faces)

octahedron (8 faces)

How to become a math consultant

"I studied mathematics at university," says Trevor. "I met people who agreed with me that math is exciting. I began thinking about how to teach math so students are not frightened by it."

After graduation, Trevor worked as a math teacher. "I loved teaching, but I really wanted to teach teachers," he laughs. "Then a consultant's job came up in the school system. It sounded perfect! I applied for the job, and got it."

Math in space

Mathematics is needed for space exploration. The design of space vehicles, the calculation of their payloads, fuels, speeds, and the paths they follow — all these depend on mathematics. The radio messages sent back to Earth, instructions from mission control, images of the solar system — none of these could be sent without mathematics.

Counting and calculating

People first learned to count in prehistoric times, and mathematics has been important ever since. Knowledge of math has been passed on from one generation to another. Long before numbers were represented by symbols, people used fingers and toes to calculate numbers. Many number systems are based on the number 10.

An abacus is a calculating device that has been used for more than 5000 years. By moving beads along the bars, you can keep track of ones, tens, hundreds, thousands, and so on. It's easy, and experienced users can add, subtract, multiply, and divide without any need for pencil and paper. In Europe the abacus was common until the 17th century; it is still used today in parts of the Middle East, Japan, and China.

Is this career for you?

A consultant in a school system must be able to work well with others. "You can't turn people off. You must be able to relate to people and accept them. Teachers have many different viewpoints, but there is no place for conflict in this process. I have to try to understand the teachers I'm working with. It can take a while for a teacher to recognize the value of a new teaching method and be willing to use it.

"Change is a slow process," says Trevor. "Teachers will not change the way they teach overnight. I have to be persistent, but in a friendly and understanding way." Trevor's employers understand that his work is a slow process. "They give us the time to discuss issues with our colleagues and figure out the best ways to improve the subject. We are dealing with ideas. Communicating these ideas to teachers so that they will adopt them takes a long time."

Good listening skills are important, too. Trevor must listen carefully to students, teachers, and parents if he really wants to help them. "After all," says Trevor, "we're all looking for the same answers. What I like most about this job is the nonstop discussion. My own education never stops. You have to be willing to change and adopt better ideas if you want to be a good math consultant."

Trevor finds it hard to think of anything he doesn't like about his career. "If a teacher doesn't want to adopt our methods, I see it as a challenge. I also like the fact that I have some freedom to work on projects of my own. I have had time to write textbooks and develop a TV program."

Career planning

Learn to write programs for computers. The logical thinking will help you understand math. Knowing how to write programs is important in many jobs.

Making Career Connections

Ask permission to do a "job shadow" with a math consultant. Follow the person for half a day, taking notes about what the job involves.

Write to a college or training program and request information about jobs that involve teaching.

Talk to someone who uses computers on the job. Ask how mathematics is related to the work.

Getting started

Interested in being a math consultant? Here's what you can do now.

1. Take math courses in high school. They are essential for any career in math or technology.
2. Offer to help younger children with their math schoolwork. Think of ways to help them understand numbers.
3. Find a book of math puzzles in the library. Puzzles make you think in new and different ways.
4. Share mathematical puzzles with your friends. Make up puzzles and try them on each other.
5. Think about the different kinds of tests you are given in your different subjects. Multiple choice tests, short answer tests, and essay tests have advantages and disadvantages.

Related careers

Here are some related careers you may want to check out.

Teacher
Teaches mathematics, including counting, measuring, and calculating. In higher grades, teaches arithmetic, geometry, algebra, trigonometry, calculus, and other kinds of math.

Human resources consultant
Assists managers in large corporations to organize effective training programs for employees.

Mathematics professor
Teaches mathematics at a college or university. Does research to develop new mathematical ideas.

Training specialist
Does on-the-job training. May teach math and computer skills to employees, or may teach managers how to use new technologies in their businesses.

Future watch

In the 21st century, knowledge of math and computers will be more important than ever. Our high-tech society needs people who understand math. So schools and school boards will want innovative people to make this subject interesting to students.

It's a Fact

In our number system — the decimal system — we can write any number using only ten digits: 0, 1, 2, 3, 4, 5, 6, 7, 8, 9. In computers, counting and calculating are done using only two digits: 0 and 1. This is called the binary system.

Catherine Lung

Computer Programmer

PERSONAL PROFILE

Career: Computer programmer. "I've always enjoyed using computers, so it seemed like a natural choice."

Interests: Music, piano, reading. "I like reading nonfiction, especially biographies."

Latest accomplishment: Translating a computer program into French and Portuguese.

Why I do what I do: "My spoken English is not the best, so I prefer to communicate with the computer; it has its own universal languages."

I am: Logical, creative, patient, and helpful.

What I wanted to be when I was in school: "I wanted to be a teacher, actually. My teachers were good role models and I thought I would follow their example."

What a computer programmer does

Without a program, a computer is just a collection of wires and electronic microchips. Someone has to tell a computer what to do and how to do it. Sets of instructions for computers are called programs. Catherine Lung is a computer programmer. She writes programs, working for a company that specializes in educational programs. Recently, she created a program that helps high school and college students learn chemistry.

Catherine's program simulates, or imitates, a chemistry experiment. In a real laboratory, some experiments are dangerous or difficult to do, and others are too expensive. On the computer screen, experiments can be exciting, but inexpensive and harmless.

A successful programmer has to be aware of the latest developments in computer technology. Computers change quickly. Hardware that was ahead of its time two years ago may be out of date now. For example, when personal computers first became popular in the 1970s, information was stored mainly on floppy disks. Then hard drives became common, because they had greater storage capacity. Now, for some purposes, these have been overtaken by compact disk (CD) drives, which have an even greater capacity. Programmers must keep up to date to take advantage of the more powerful devices as they become available.

Part of a program written in BASIC. "Think of it as a code, or a new language," says Catherine.

```
10    ON ERROR GOTO 999
20    OPEN "A", #1, "NAMES"
110   REM      add new entries to file
120   INPUT  "NAME";N$        'Start of Loop
130   IF N$="" THEN 300       'Carriage Return Exits Loop
140   LINE INPUT  "ADDRESS? ";A$
150   LINE INPUT  "BIRTHDAY? ";B$
160   PRINT #1,N$
170   PRINT #1,A$
180   PRINT #1,B$
190   PRINT:  GOTO 120        'End of Loop
300   CLOSE #1
999   ON ERROR GOTO 0
```

Fact or fiction?

Computer-controlled robots can be readily programmed to perform repetitive tasks such as welding on an assembly line. Computers can also store information and calculate at superhuman speeds. But a computer's "thoughts" are limited to the program that controls it. The advanced robots that you see in movies are only fiction. A computer-controlled robot that can move like a human is still a long way off.

Techie talk

Techie (pronounced "teckie"): a person who enjoys and understands the details of computer technology

Hardware: the parts of a computer, such as the processing unit, screen, keyboard, and printer

Program: a set of instructions for the computer. (These may be written in several different languages, such as BASIC, Cobol, Fortran, Pascal, and C.)

Software: a set of instructions for the computer (same as "program")

Byte: an amount of computer memory; enough to store one symbol, such as A, a, 2, $, or Z

Kilobyte: 1024 bytes

"K": short for "kilobytes of memory." (Home computers might have from 512 K to 8000 K memory. Large mainframe computers might have as much as 500 000 000 K.)

Simulation: imitation. (For example, flight simulation programs imitate how an airplane functions. You act as pilot, while your screen shows you the view from the cockpit.)

Machine code: very detailed programming language. (Any language used by a programmer is translated into this machine language within the computer.)

All in a day's work

A lot of us were introduced to computers through computer games. In these games, the computer responds to the player's moves, so there is real interaction. Because they are interactive, computer games can be challenging to players at all levels. For the same reason, computers can have a much wider use, as educators.

Computers have been in schools for some time. At first, you had to be in a computer science class to use one. Now, computers are important in other subjects as well. With advanced graphics, sound, and movement, they can create realistic images on the screen. Simulation of real activities becomes possible.

Simulated chemistry

Catherine Lung's employer is a company that was formed by a group of chemistry professors. They wanted students to be able to plan *and carry out* chemistry experiments while sitting at a computer. That is, they saw a need for a program to simulate a chemistry laboratory.

Catherine was one of the programmers hired for the project. The program creates a large building containing different kinds of chemistry labs, storerooms, libraries, and workrooms. It takes students through a storeroom, where they pick up chemicals and equipment they need. There are test tubes, flasks, bottles, chemicals, electronic measuring devices, and more. Then the students go to the appropriate lab to conduct the experiment. In this way, they can try things out for themselves, even making "explosions" that would be too dangerous to do in a real lab.

Dedicated teamwork

It takes determination to get a program to work. "I work with a team of other programmers to create this software," says Catherine. "Even with many people on the project, it takes a long time. There are three kinds of labs and the programming took a year for each. We're hoping to add to the program in the future." The programmers help each other with constructive criticism and creative suggestions. Individuals work on parts of the program, but it takes a team to complete the whole project.

Catherine and her fellow programmers also meet with the teachers and students who use their program. "We've had mostly positive feedback," says Catherine. "The program doesn't give all the answers. Students have to do their own analysis. Teachers like the fact that this program motivates students to learn. Students like it because it's fun."

Computer programming involves a lot of work on your own. However, other programmers may have ideas that can help you solve a problem.

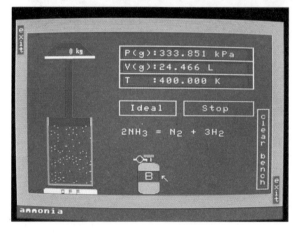

Scene from *The Electric Chemistry Building*, a program that Catherine worked on. High school students use this program to simulate laboratory experiments.

Virus!

Have you had a virus recently? If you've had a cold or a bout of flu, the answer is yes. A virus is a tiny particle that manages to get inside living cells. Once inside, it takes over the cell and produces many copies of itself. While this is going on in your body, you may have a fever or a cough or just feel sick.

A computer virus acts in a similar way. As it is passed from disk to disk, or from computer to computer, it reproduces itself. It causes damage, or at least a disturbance, wherever it goes.

What does a computer virus look like? It's simply a little bit of code. The illustration shows some machine code — actual instructions for the computer. A virus could be hidden anywhere in here. Finding it is like looking for a needle in a haystack!

What does a virus do, besides reproduce itself? It might destroy all information in a computer's memory. It might destroy data files stored on disks. It might flash a message on the screen that disrupts a program and forces the operator to start the work all over again. Or it might do nothing at all until something activates it. A few lines of code can cause a lot of headaches for people who rely on computers.

How does a virus get started? Someone writes the virus program and attaches it to a program on a floppy disk. When someone copies the program from the disk or over a telephone line, the virus is copied as well. The virus can be passed to more and more computers in the same way. An undetected virus can spread to thousands of computers. Fortunately, there are now programs available that seek out and destroy viruses before they can do any damage.

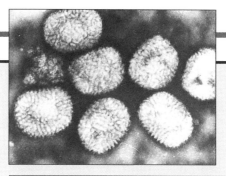

Virus particles, such as those that might give you an illness, magnified by an electron microscope.

Machine code. A virus could be hidden in a single line or in several lines.

```
3447:0100    46 F0 01 06 74 E9 01 06-8C E9 81 3E 8C E9 FF 00
3447:0110    7E 06 C7 06 8C E9 FF 00-81 3E 74 E9 34 00 36 34
3447:0120    A1 3E E9 A3 B4 C6 C7 06-3E E9 FF FF C6 06 56 E9
3447:0130    03 E9 A5 02 83 7E F6 00-B8 00 00 75 01 40 8B D0
3447:0140    B8 1C 00 8B CA F7 26 70-DE 96 8B 84 A4 C6 3B 06
3447:0150    68 E9 BA 00 00 7C 01 42-22 CA B8 1C 00 F7 26 70
3447:0160    DE 96 8B 84 A4 C6 3B 06-80 E9 BA 00 00 7F 01 42
3447:0170    22 CA B8 1C 00 F7 26 70-DE 96 8B 84 A4 C6 3B 06
```

Activity

Logical thinking

Programmers must often solve puzzles. Programmers have to tell the computer how to do something. In so doing, they have to give short, one-at-a-time instructions. Here's a puzzle for you to try, one step at a time.

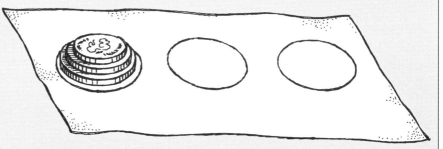

You will need
three coins of different sizes
   (for example, a quarter, nickel, and dime)
piece of plain paper
pencil

1. On the paper, draw three circles, as shown. In the first circle, pile up the coins, with the largest on the bottom and the smallest on the top.

2. Move all the coins to the third circle, still with the largest on the bottom and the smallest on top. There are two rules.
   ■ You may only move the top coin at any one time.
   ■ You may never place a larger coin over a smaller one.

3. What is the smallest number of moves that you need to do this? (Answer is on page 48.)

4. Set yourself the same puzzle, with four different-sized coins and three circles. What is the smallest number of moves needed to move all the coins to the third circle?

5. Try the same puzzle with five coins and three circles. Do you begin to see a pattern in the moves?

6. Write step-by-step instructions for a friend. Have your friend follow the instructions — see if they work.

How to become a computer programmer

Catherine went to high school in Hong Kong. In her school, she had to choose between two disciplines: arts and science. "I preferred mathematics and logical thinking," says Catherine. "I did enjoy literature and history, but science seemed like the way to go." Then she started working with computers and felt they were what she was looking for.

After completing high school in Hong Kong, Catherine came to North America for further education. "Everyday language was a barrier for me at first. I took English lessons, and still do. But math and science are universal languages; there is no barrier to understanding.

"In my first year, I took general studies. I had courses in algebra, calculus, physics, chemistry, and computer science. For the next three years," Catherine says, "I took a lot of courses in computer hardware and software. I learned about computer components and how they interact. I also studied computer architecture — computer structure and design. To write software, I needed to know different computer languages, such as Fortran, Cobol, Pascal, and C." Each language uses its own symbols and codes to instruct the computer.

In Catherine's final year, she had to write a major computer program. "I needed to find a professor to sponsor my project. One of the chemistry professors was working on a program, and I became involved with that. In fact, it was this same professor who started the company I work for. After I graduated, he invited me to work for the company and continue the project."

Is this career for you?

"Programming requires a lot of patience," says Catherine. "It seems there are always bugs in the program. It takes time to fix all these small errors, so you can spend long hours working alone. I enjoy this because I'm a quiet person and feel comfortable at the computer. But when I've got a deadline and I'm delayed by problems, it can get pretty tense."

In this job, you must be willing to keep learning. "I'm curious about new technologies. It helps me in my career to keep myself informed of the latest developments. I read computer magazines and technical papers so I'll have a better insight into computers." Catherine has taken the time to go back to school and get another degree in computer engineering. "I like to learn; I want to explore my potential."

Programmers need to be able to think logically, but be creative at the same time. Programmers have a lot of independence in their work. They can decide when and how to work on different parts of their job. But there is a certain amount of interaction with other programmers. Catherine says, "I need feedback from co-workers if I want to learn things about my work. They tell me what they think of my program, and I can use their ideas to improve it."

There's a bug in the program!

What is a "bug" to you? A beetle, an ant, a "true bug," or any kind of creepy crawly? A bug in a program is something different — it's an error in the code that prevents the program from working properly. The illustration shows a small piece of a program written in Pascal. These code words tell the computer to sort some numbers. For example, "37, 9 , 59, 16," would be sorted into order from smallest to largest: 9, 16, 37, 59. But there's a bug in this program! In the first line, there's a typing error. Instead of sorting all the numbers (from "upper bound" to "lower bound"), the program will sort all but the last number. This will cause an error in the printout for some groups of numbers, but not for all. Finding a bug like this, which causes occasional errors, can be very tricky.

```
BEGIN
    FOR  j := upper_bound DOWNTO lower_bound + 2 DO
      FOR  i := lower_bound TO j - 1 DO
        IF ((values[row][i] > values[row][j]) AND (is_ascending) ) THEN
          exchange_values ( values[row][i], values[row][j] )
        ELSE
        IF ((values[row][i] < values[row][j]) AND (NOT is_ascending) ) THEN
          exchange_values ( values[row][i], values[row][j] );
END;    { bubble_sort }
```

The bug in this Pascal program is a single digit that was typed incorrectly. The "2" in the first line should be a "1."

Career planning

Making Career Connections

Invite a computer programmer to your school to talk about different kinds of programming jobs.

At your school, find out which institutions in your area offer courses in programming. Write to one of them, asking about their entrance requirements.

Visit a library and check out books on computers. Make a list of the different uses of computers. Then make a list of the ways they affect your life.

In a daily newspaper, find the "Help Wanted" section. From the advertisements for programmers, make a list of all the programming languages that are mentioned.

Getting started

Interested in being a computer programmer? Here's what you can do now.

1. Take many science, math, and computer courses in high school. A lot of programming is based on a good knowledge of math and logic.
2. Use computers as much as possible. See if you like working with them.
3. Read magazine articles about computers. You can learn how they work and see how computer technology is advancing.
4. Browse in computer stores. See what kinds of software and hardware are available.

Related careers

Here are some related careers you may want to check out.

Maintenance programmer
Maintains, fixes, and enhances existing programs in large companies.

Systems analyst
Works with companies that are planning to become computerized. Helps them decide what particular system would be appropriate for that company. Chooses software and hardware to go with that system. Helps to educate employees about how they will use the computers.

Computer games designer
Designs and programs video games. May work for a games company or may work independently and attempt to sell the product.

Real-time programmer
Writes programs for applications such as a robot on an assembly line, an automated warehouse, or an automatic teller machine.

Future watch

Computers are used in stores, banks, cars, businesses, homes, games, and appliances, and will be even more common in the future. Programming skills will be useful in many careers. Designers, artists, doctors, teachers, business people, musicians, accountants, lawyers, scientists, engineers — all of these people might write programs for their own professions. As well, programmers with hobbies or outside interests may find that their programming skills allow them to move into new fields.

Juliana Fonagy

Interior Designer

PERSONAL PROFILE

Career: Interior designer. "I like working with computers, even though I'm an artist at heart."

Interests: Knitting, painting, reading, going to auctions, buying antiques. "And I'm engaged to be married."

Latest accomplishment: Using a computer to draw the furniture layouts for some law offices.

Why I do what I do: "I always liked art and I was interested in playing around with room arrangements. I used to watch that old TV show 'Rhoda.' She was an interior designer and I remember thinking that I wanted to do the same thing."

I am: Friendly, determined, and sometimes aggressive.

What I wanted to be when I was in school: "I wanted to do something involving interior design. I gave some thought to being an art or design teacher, but I really wanted to work in the field."

What an interior designer does

The environment where people work is an important aspect of any job. Everyone needs fresh air, proper lighting, tolerable noise levels, and a comfortable place to sit or stand. Equipment, such as a photocopier, should be placed where it is needed, so workers don't waste time whenever they use it. Designing workplaces that are pleasant and efficient is the job of an interior designer. In addition to offices, interior designers might design hospitals, restaurants, factories, or people's homes.

Juliana Fonagy is a computer-assisted interior designer. She works for a company that designs restaurants and offices. In the past, design drawings were done by hand and took a very long time, but Juliana uses a computer to make her job easier. She uses AUTOCAD, a software package that allows her to draw and design on a computer screen. AUTOCAD stands for AUTOmated Computer Assisted Drafting and Design. "The computer makes the drawings more quickly, but there is still a lot of creativity involved. No two interior design jobs are the same," Juliana explains.

Cutting down repetition

A designer using AUTOCAD takes an architect's drawings and transfers them onto the computer. Furniture, partitions, electrical outlets, and lighting fixtures are then added to the drawing. "We have a library of details on the computer," explains Juliana. "It saves us a lot of repetitive drawing. For example, things like countertops, soundproofed walls, and storage space are on file in the computer's memory. We just call them up on screen and position them in the drawing. In the past, each part of the drawing had to be added by hand. "

Increasing accuracy

Computers are also more exact when it comes to measurement. If someone designs an interior but has the wrong room dimensions, the client might end up with a very cramped work space or extra, wasted space. "In one project we worked on recently," recalls Juliana, "the architects started working on the computer, but ran out of money. Producing drawings on the computer is expensive. They had to finish the drawings by hand. When we got the drawings, we found a lot of errors. The work done on the computer didn't match up with the hand drawings. Errors can happen on the computer, too, but they are a lot more likely to occur when drawing is done by hand.

"Basically what we do is copy the floor plan given to us by the architect," says Juliana. "We just keep adding more and more details until the drawing is complete." Then the drawings are passed on to the builders who will do the actual construction.

Juliana enjoys working with computers despite the fact that she is an artist at heart. "I don't know what's inside the computer or how it works, but I can use it. I know how to run the program. And, to say the least, it makes my job easier and more enjoyable."

WEST VALLEY MIDDLE

Designing for humans: ergonomics

Machines are operated by humans, workplaces are occupied by humans, and products are used by humans. Specialists in ergonomics — human factors engineering — are experts in designs that suit human needs.

Consumer products, for example, need to suit the users. Bicycles are adjustable to fit the size of the rider. Car phones can be operated with only one hand. Kitchen counters are at a convenient level for people of average height. Products for elderly people and others are designed for any special needs.

If products are designed with people in mind, they are easier to use, workplaces and homes are more pleasant, and machines are more efficient.

What improvements have been made in the design of modern telephones?

All in a day's work

"I don't really have a set schedule," says Juliana. "It's not a traditional nine-to-five kind of job. The time I spend on a project on any given day depends on the deadline. I could be working on a project that is due on a Friday. Other clients might walk in on Tuesday and say they need their drawings the next day. Usually I'll give the new job a shot if the request is reasonable. So sometimes I'll end up working late hours to get things done on time."

Fortunately for Juliana, computer technology speeds up the drawing process. "Things have become so competitive that we'll take jobs that must be done much sooner than we'd like," explains Juliana. "Before, we would refuse a job if the client wanted the work done in six months or less. It was simply not enough time for us to do a good job. Now we'll take jobs that a client wants done in only four months."

Juliana will take an architect's drawing like this and transfer it onto a computer. She can then make changes and add details with the AUTOCAD program.

Using the computer

On a typical day, Juliana might be working at the computer, putting in all the doors on a drawing. "I use a program called 'Doors'; it's part of AUTOCAD. It lets me choose the sizes of doors and position them on the drawing. If the client decides later that we are going to use doors of a different width, I simply press a couple of keys on the computer and a new door will be inserted into the drawing. The drawing can then be printed out with all the new doors in place. You can see the advantage this program gives us. Without it, the architects would have to erase every door and redraw them by hand."

AUTOCAD is a detailed program and it takes time to learn how to use it. "Some people find the system frustrating," says Juliana, "but I enjoy it. I've spent so much time using this program that I'm familiar with how it works. Practice makes perfect!"

Meetings

Juliana doesn't spend all her time working alone with a computer. Far from it! She also does a lot of work with other people. Designing interiors is a complex and demanding job. It takes a team of well-trained individuals to do a job, and to do it on time. "There are several people involved with each project. There are project managers and directors, architectural technicians, designers, and AUTOCAD operators."

Juliana and her co-workers share ideas and help each other solve problems.

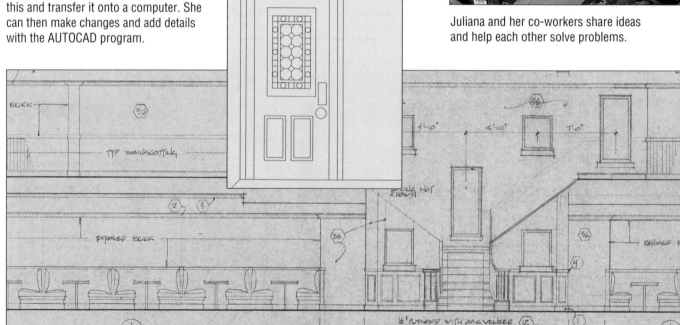

Designers choose colors and furniture and design a layout; they are responsible for the "look" the client wants. If the client wants red walls, the designer includes red walls and uses other colors to produce a pleasing final effect. "I want to get more involved in the design of the layouts in the future," says Juliana.

There are also team meetings that she has to attend. As she explains, "We get together and brainstorm, trade information, and decide on a plan of attack. We figure out what has to be done, who will do what, and when it should be finished. Good communication skills are important in these meetings. To cooperate with others, you need to understand what they are saying. You have to be able to make yourself understood, too."

Designing interiors involves teamwork. Each person has unique skills that are required if the team is to do a good job.

In the past, Juliana did not have much contact with clients. Only the senior members of the team were involved in the client relations. "Now, with tighter time lines, our whole team will sometimes meet with clients. It's easier for all of us to get the information firsthand. This makes sense because it saves time and we get a clearer idea of what the client wants."

Seeing a completed interior is a satisfying experience for the people who designed it.

Inspecting sites

Juliana's job may require a trip to the building site to check up on the work in progress. "This is one of the most enjoyable aspects of my job. It's fun to see a room being built, especially one that I knew as drawings on paper." Juliana inspects the work being done. She may spot a problem the builders overlooked.

A trip to the job site can require a sense of humor. "I once went to a construction site downtown. I had to wear a construction hat and boots as a safety precaution. The funny thing was, I was dressed for the office. I hadn't expected to go to the site that day and I was wearing a black miniskirt. I got a lot of funny looks from passersby, to say the least. One curious person asked me if I was really a construction worker."

Activity

Designing an interior

You will need
measuring stick or measuring tape
paper and pencil
graph paper

1. Measure the dimensions of a room in your home and the furniture in it. As you do this, write down the accurate measurements on a sketch of the room.

2. On the graph paper, make an accurate scaled drawing of the room.

3. Redesign your room. Move things around or add furniture to the room. Use your imagination to improve it as much as you can.

4. What type of workplaces are you interested in — laboratories, offices, restaurants, warehouses, factories, schools? Use your imagination to draw a plan of your ideal workplace.

How to become an interior designer

Juliana's career really began back in high school. "I took some architecture courses involving interior design. I really enjoyed them and did well in them. I was pretty sure that I wanted a career in this field." Luckily for Juliana, her school also offered a co-op program. This enabled students to work every other day at a job where they earned school credits instead of money. "I did co-op in my last year of high school. I worked for an interior design company. It was a great experience. I learned more about design and discovered what life in this field is like. I was sure I wanted to pursue this career. After I finished high school, the company asked me to stay on for the summer and I gladly accepted the offer. That certainly helped me to get my present job."

After high school, Juliana went to college for three years, where she studied interior design, also called "environmental design." "I hadn't worked with computers in my co-op job, but I could see the value they would have in the design industry. So I signed up for all the AUTOCAD courses. But new versions of AUTOCAD are released periodically. This means I have to stay tuned to the latest changes in the software. In this respect, my education doesn't stop. I'm always learning more."

Becoming qualified is only the first step

Juliana admits that landing her present job involved a little luck. "I was in the right place at the right time," she says. But her previous work in interior design and her ability to use computers qualified her for the job. "My college instructor, who also taught my present AUTOCAD department manager, suggested that I give him a call. I applied for a job, and after several interviews I got it."

With a computer and appropriate software, you can draw and save pictures like this one.

Is this career for you?

Juliana feels that interior design is a great career for people who love art and are creative. "I wanted a career involving both art and design. Solving space problems, deciding how to use space, and figuring out better ways of arranging furniture in that space — these are things I really enjoy."

A little patience doesn't hurt. "Sometimes you work hard for hours and then find you've made a mistake. You need to get yourself over the hurdle and on to the next challenge." There is also a lot of routine work. When a client wants a standard arrangement, the designers don't have much room for creativity, but the next project might be entirely different.

Mistakes are inevitable. "We're all human. But in my work, errors can be very costly," says Juliana. "The drawings are expensive to produce because they take a lot of time and they're done on high-tech equipment. Redrawing them can be a real headache. The architectural technicians check my drawings and point out any errors, but I want them to be as error-free as possible."

Deadlines can be a problem, putting pressure on the designers. "I don't like it when time lines are tight and we run into problems. Sometimes it feels like we're running into brick walls and not making progress. Some clients have trouble making decisions. One client decided he wanted a new design after construction had begun! It can get pretty frustrating. But if we pull together as a team, we eventually get the project finished."

The most satisfying part of the job is inspecting the interior when the construction is completed. "Checking out the finished job is quite a thrill," says Juliana.

Career planning

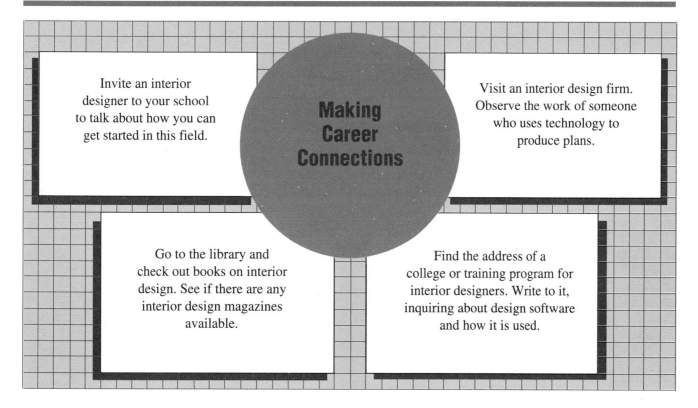

Making Career Connections

Invite an interior designer to your school to talk about how you can get started in this field.

Visit an interior design firm. Observe the work of someone who uses technology to produce plans.

Go to the library and check out books on interior design. See if there are any interior design magazines available.

Find the address of a college or training program for interior designers. Write to it, inquiring about design software and how it is used.

Getting started

Interested in being an interior designer or an AUTOCAD operator? Here's what you can do now.

1. Take architecture and interior design courses in high school.
2. You should take math courses as well. Architecture and design involve calculation and measurement.
3. If your school has any draw or paint programs for computers, get permission to use them in your free time. See what you can produce using this type of software.
4. Whenever possible, use a computer to do calculations or word processing. You need to be able to use a computer as a tool to help you with your work.
5. Take art courses; they'll help you become more creative.

Related careers

Here are some related careers you may want to check out.

Architect

Designs buildings that people will live and work in, including structures as small as sheds or as large as skyscrapers. Designs buildings that are functional, safe, and pleasing to the eye.

Furniture designer

Designs and builds furniture for homes and offices. A creative field, requiring imagination as well as artistic skills.

This chair was designed and constructed in China more than 2000 years ago. Designers' tools and techniques have changed, but artistic skills remain central to this career.

Future watch

Computers are revolutionizing architecture and design. Jobs can be done more efficiently and more accurately using computers. If you have computer experience, an employer will choose you over someone who has none. In this industry, the future is brightest for those who are familiar with computers and who are willing to keep learning on the job.

Herminio Fernandes

Video Games Programmer

PERSONAL PROFILE

Career: Video games programmer. "Designing games is a lot of fun; it's like creating your own little movie."

Interests: Cycling, cars, spending time with friends, camping.

Latest accomplishment: Writing a program that helps artists assemble the pictures for video games.

Why I do what I do: "I started writing computer games early in high school. I really enjoyed what I was doing, so I stuck with it."

I am: Determined, creative, logical, and occasionally stubborn.

What I wanted to be when I was in school: "I wanted to be a games programmer when I was in high school. Programming has always interested me and I enjoy the flexibility this career offers."

What a video games programmer does

In the 1970s, video games became a popular form of entertainment. Today, video games are more popular than ever with both children and adults. And with the improvements in computer technology, video games will become even more complex and challenging in the future.

Programming a video game is no easy task. It often takes a team of people to complete a game and get it in the stores. Herminio Fernandes is a member of this team. He's a games programmer. "I began writing and selling video games on my own when I was in high school," says Herminio.

You've probably played video games, so you know how complex they can be. A video games programmer has to figure out how a game will work. The programmer must develop a script, just like a movie script, that outlines what will happen in each stage of the game. It's a very time-consuming process.

Next comes the programming. The programmer must type in all the instructions that tell the computer what to do. "I think the hardest part of designing a game is programming the computer's strategy," says Herminio. "You can't have the same thing happening over and over. That would make the game predictable and boring. So I have to program a lot of variation into the game.

"Video games offer a programmer many options. I can work on sports games, action-adventure games, or educational games. The process of programming is similar with all of them, but different types of games allow me to use my imagination in different ways.

"I'm looking forward to using the technology of the future. Graphics and sound will be more realistic. Games will also be more interactive. You'll use more of your body to play a game. For instance, you might wear a helmet with built-in video screens, one in front of each eye. Or you might wear gloves so that you can move your hands to control some of the more complex games. The possibilities are endless."

These lines make up part of the code that tells a computer what to do.

```
repeat
     Circ( random(getmaxX)+1, random(getmaxY)+1, positive,
          random(getmaxcolor), happy );
     setcolor(yellow);
     outtextXY(x-30, y-100, 'You WIN !');
until keypressed;
```

Herminio checks out the latest video games.

Addicted to fun

Walk by any video arcade and you'll see many people, of all ages, glued to their favorite games.

But there is a problem with the popularity of video games. Games can become habit-forming, time-consuming, and expensive.

Sometimes drastic steps have been taken to try to solve this problem. In 1980, the council of a small town decided to remove all video games from the arcades. Apparently the children played the games constantly. But the plan didn't work. The kids simply rode their bikes to the arcade in the next county to play the games.

Video games *are* fun. But treat your playing time like money in the bank. Don't spend it all in one place.

All in a day's work

Most games on the market are designed by groups of people, not by a single individual. Video games publishers, the large companies that produce and sell the games, pay for these projects. They gather a team together and tell them what they want.

Artists draw the characters and background scenes and choose the colors in the game. Meanwhile, programmers, like Herminio, program the movement of the characters, the rules of the game, how a game moves on the screen, how the characters interact, and the strategies that the computer will use.

Designing and programming a video game require a lot of hard work. "If you don't plan the game in great detail before programming begins, you can waste a lot of time on unexpected problems."

There are different kinds of video game systems — the games you find in an arcade, and the games that you hook up to your TV set or computer screen. Herminio writes most of his programs for systems that hook up to a TV. "We design the games so they will fit on a cartridge that can be plugged into the system. There are

It's a Fact

The new "virtual reality" games, with 3-D images, are highly realistic. As you play, you seem to be part of a movie on the screen, and you can affect the outcome of the plot.

limits to what the systems can handle. We can only put so much information on a cartridge. So we have to design games that suit the system."

The artists and programmers work at the same time. "I usually work faster than the artists. So, I go ahead with the programming before the characters have been designed. Instead of a spaceship on the screen, which the artists are still designing, I'll have a piece of junk. This way I can work out the movement and logic of the game while the artists work on the visual details. When they are finished, I get the data and put their pictures in my program."

A single video game can involve more than one programmer. Herminio's latest project is an action-adventure game based on a cartoon series. "I'm working on all the exterior stuff. I do all the action that takes place outdoors. Another programmer is working on the parts where the character runs around indoors. When the character lands a plane and enters a building, the other program takes over. When the

character leaves the building, my program starts up again. When the two programs are combined, we have a complete game."

Call the exterminator!

"Finishing a game is difficult," says Herminio. "A lot of little things need fixing. There are always bugs in the program; they're a real pain." (To find out what a bug is, see "There's a bug in the program!" on page 26.) For instance, you may have played a game where a character freezes and you can no longer control it. A bug in the program might cause this. "A game can take months to complete in the final stages because of bugs. This can be frustrating, but I'm always determined to sort out the problems and finish the game."

Once the game is totally debugged and approved, Herminio sends it to the publishers. They spend hours playing the game, testing it to see if there are any problems. "If they find any problems, they reject the game and we have to do more work on it. Some publishers can be really picky. They want the game to be perfect. Other publishers just want to get the game in the stores as soon as they can.

"It's great when the game is finally in the stores. Then I can turn my attention to my next project."

Programmers can't always wait for artists to finish their designs before they begin programming. They may use substitute shapes in their programs until the artists finish designing the characters.

Activity

Games of chance and challenge

Chance or "luck" is a part of many games. In some games, such as Snakes and Ladders®, dice are rolled. Winning at these games is a matter of chance. In other games, such as checkers or chess, winning is a matter of skill rather than chance. All kinds of games — video games, computer games, card games, sports, pencil-and-paper games — can exercise your brain.

1. Think of all the video games or computer games that you know. What kinds of games are there? Think of at least three kinds; then make a list of the games of each type. (There are many ways to do this. Read on to get some ideas.)

2. Some games depend on chance, and some don't. In your favorite game, how much chance is involved? Can the way you play change how the game progresses? Or does the game always progress in the same way, no matter what you do? Is the original setup always the same, or does it vary? List 10 games in order, from the one where luck is most involved, to the one where luck has the least influence. (In your list, include all kinds of games, not just video games or computer games.)

3. Quick reflexes are necessary in many sports and games, such as baseball and hockey. In some video and computer games, you also need quick reflexes. For some of these, quick reflexes are everything — you hardly need to think; list at least five games like this.

List another five where both thinking skills and quick reflexes are important. Think of a game in which quick reflexes are not involved, but in which you get as much time as you want for each move. Which of these three types do you prefer, and why?

4. People have always played games. Two-player games, such as Battleship, Hangman, and many card games, have been popular for generations. Many of these have been adapted as computer games. Now you can choose to play them alone on the computer, or with a friend. If you have a computer available at your school or community center, select one example of this type of game. Play it several times on the computer, then play it several times with a friend using pencil and paper and no computer. Did the computer enrich the game? If so, what did it add? What are some advantages of playing with people? What are some advantages of playing with the computer?

How to become a video games programmer

"I've always loved playing video games," says Herminio. "I was also curious to find out how they worked. I wrote my first game on a personal computer when I was 12 years old."

On his own, Herminio learned different computer languages. He was his own teacher and student. "I never took computer courses. I read books on computer programming," he says. "Computer courses would have been a waste of time for me, but if you are interested in learning about computers, a computer course would be a great place to start."

Herminio continued writing games throughout high school. When he wrote two games that were sold to a video games publisher, he realized he could make a career out of his hobby.

"I kept buying better computers because I could write better games with them." Eventually, Herminio was approached to do some work on

cartridge games for home game consoles. "I've been working with the same people for a few years now." Herminio is continuing his work on game cartridges but would like to try something different in the future.

"There's a lot of money in cartridge games, but I would like to create a game on a personal computer. Size is less of a limitation. Personal computers give you a lot more freedom to create."

Art and technology

Video games programmers get most of the credit when a game becomes popular. They're the ones who figure out what a game is going to do. But the way it looks depends on both the programmer and the artists involved. Video games artists draw all the characters and scenes for a game. Programmers tell them what they want, how big the characters should be, and then let them go to it.

Each frame is drawn by hand, like a cartoon. Then a device called a scanner converts the picture into a set of electronic signals. These

signals are the code that the computer recognizes. The programmer then inserts the drawing into the program and animates it.

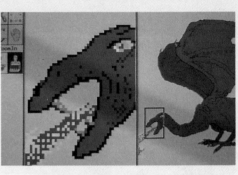

Depending on the type of screen you use, pictures in a video game may appear to be made up of tiny squares.

Is this career for you?

A lot of people love video games, but most don't have the knowledge or patience to write one themselves. If you're creative, enjoy solving problems, and can think logically, you might like programming video games. "Programming requires attention to detail," says Herminio. "I have to admit that bugs in the program can drive me nuts. It can get very frustrating. But it's a big part of programming and you have to live with it.

"My career involves a lot of organizing. You can't rush a project and expect your program to work." Herminio has to keep lists and set up a schedule for himself so he'll get things done on time. "I always have a lot of ideas. But I have to write them down so I don't forget them."

The artists and programmers don't always see eye to eye. This can be frustrating, but they have to get together and sort out any difficulties so they can finish the game on schedule.

"I enjoy working whenever I want," says Herminio. "I don't have to work nine-to-five. As long as I have a computer system, I can work anywhere. And I enjoy seeing my name on a game cartridge in a store."

One of the advantages of Herminio's job is that he can do his work at home.

Career planning

Making Career Connections

At a library, examine a list of computer-related occupations. Find out what education and training are required for each type of job.

What kind of part-time jobs would help you learn about programming and computers? Try to find someone who has such a job, and interview the person. Afterward, list the advantages and disadvantages of the job.

Find the address of a college near you that offers computer training. Write to the college, asking what course of study would help you to become a video games programmer.

Write to a computer company or a software company. Ask for information about different types of jobs in the computer field.

Getting started

Interested in being a video games programmer? Here's what you can do now.

1. Learn about computers. Get to know how they work, inside and out.
2. Compare games from the 1980s with the games you see today. Find out the technical reasons why the games now have better color and better action.
3. Try writing programs on a computer. Make this a hobby.
4. Learn about electronics by taking electronics courses in high school.

Related careers

Here are some related careers you may want to check out.

Video games artist
Designs characters and scenery for video games. Works with other artists and games programmers.

Process control programmer
Writes programs used for applications such as robotics, manufacturing, warehousing, mining, automated machine tools, and traffic control systems.

As today's preschoolers grow up, the market for video games will continue to expand.

Catherine Chandler-Crichlow — High-Tech Adult Educator

When today's adults were in school, no one could imagine what business would be like in the 21st century. Because the technology used in business changes so quickly, everyone needs to keep learning on the job. Continuous learning is essential for a company's survival.

Catherine Chandler-Crichlow works for an organization that provides financial assistance to companies to develop training programs using new computer technologies. These programs can be used to train adults in any workplace. With degrees in both science and education, Catherine ensures that the training is high-quality, easy to use, and adaptable.

As a consultant, Catherine decides whether a company should receive money to develop a particular program. Recently, a company came to her with a plan to develop training in health and safety. Trainees would learn how to store, handle, use, and dispose of chemicals without harming themselves or the environment. In this case, the company decided to use CD-ROM technology to teach the courses. They could provide a

complete chemical encyclopedia on one disk. "We invested heavily in that company," recalls Catherine.

"To be good at this job, I need to be aware of all the changes in new technologies. I go to trade shows and I often visit companies to see their new training programs, which might be developed on CDI , DVI, or multimedia. I also read computer magazines to try to understand how technologies could be used to make learning easier for everyone."

Telephones were once the most up-to-date technology. In 1943, many people worked in offices like this one.

Catherine must keep learning on the job. Before she can help people use new technologies, she must understand them herself.

Alphabet soup

What words do these technological short forms represent? (Answers are on page 48.)

TV:	Uncommon when your grandparents were young.
LP:	Supplies 30 minutes or more of continuous music.
VCR:	Rare in homes in the 1970s, but common in the 1990s.
CD:	A replacement for LPs.
PC:	Has revolutionized workplaces, and is useful in homes and schools as well.
CD-ROM:	May replace massive reference books.
CDI:	A replacement for video cassettes.
DVI:	An improvement on CDI.
AI:	Using this, computers may be able to "think."

Getting started

1. Read avidly. Keep yourself informed of the technology that is available in the workplace.
2. Be curious. Think about how technology can help people learn and work.
3. Take math, science, and computer courses in school.
4. Visit a science museum and concentrate on the exhibits that demonstrate new technologies.

Jonathan Cullis — Research Analyst in Foreign Exchange Markets

Jonathan Cullis works for a firm that is involved with the buying and selling of foreign exchange currencies. "Investors give us money and expect us to use that money to make more. We do this by observing the value of currencies around the world. If we predict that a particular currency, say Swiss francs, or German marks, or Japanese yen, is about to go up in value, we buy some and make a profit when it goes up. It's like the stock market."

How does Jonathan's firm keep track of currency values? And how does the firm predict the future value of a foreign currency? With computers, of course.

Jonathan's computer is hooked up to a "line data feed." When changes occur in stock markets around the world, he knows about them immediately.

In foreign exchange markets, no real paper money changes hands. Buying and selling is done electronically on computers.

The advantages of technology

"I use a computer eight hours a day," says Jonathan. "We've designed a program that tracks currency values around the world, as the values change from second to second. The program decides when to buy and sell, based on this data. It's fully automated. There is so much data needed to make a decision that we use a computer to process it. Currency values can change so rapidly, it takes a computer's speed to keep up and capitalize on a situation."

Jonathan studied business and finance for four years after finishing high school. His first job was selling insurance, but he was always interested in the stock market. "Anyone can get involved in the stock market or currency trading, but there is always a risk. You need to know about handling finances."

Getting started

1. Take math and computer courses in school. These are essential for anyone interested in the world of business.
2. If you have a computer, try to find a stock market program to use on it. There are many stock market simulation games available in stores.
3. Arrange to visit a stock exchange on your own or with your school. Watch the trading "on the floor."
4. Read the business section in your daily newspaper. Track how foreign exchange rates change from day to day.
5. Check out books and magazines on the business world. There are many different business-related careers.

International exchange rates

When one nation buys something from another, payment is in the currency of the selling country. For example, when a car dealer buys Japanese cars, it pays not in dollars, but in yen. The yen are bought from a bank. The relative value of dollars and yen is called the exchange rate. Depending on the international situation, exchange rates may rise or fall. As the rates change, investors buy or sell currencies. A sample day is shown below.

Country	Monetary unit	Units per U.S. dollar
Canada	dollar	1.38
Germany	mark	1.92
Great Britain	pound	0.67
Japan	yen	157.93
Laos	kip	35.00
Pakistan	rupee	16.81

Rob Dueckman — Computer Service Technician

"You name it, I do it," says Rob Dueckman. Rob works for a chain of stores as a computer service technician. "I help consumers get their computer systems operating. I help them understand how their system works and what it can do. I also give seminars on how to use computers. Sometimes I write programs for our own office to help us operate more efficiently."

Anyone can sell a computer, even someone who doesn't really know how it works. But when customers call up with problems, only service technicians like Rob can answer their questions. "Because computers are getting cheaper, a lot more people are using them. People who aren't computer-literate need more help setting up and operating their computers," Rob explains.

Rob has always enjoyed taking apart electronic equipment.

The job

"I work at a kind of central control," says Rob. "We have smaller stores in different areas, but they all get their equipment through us."

The first thing Rob does when he arrives at work each day is to check the sales records. The company needs to know what they've sold and how much money they've made on those sales. Rob then ensures that this information is sent to all the stores. At each store, they must know what equipment they'll be getting. The central office finds out if there is any equipment that will be late in arriving. "On our computer system, we get an update of the inventory files at all the stores. We want to know what they have on the shelves and what we need to order for them."

Later, Rob is usually out on the road checking problems for customers. The problem might be with the software (the program), the hardware (the disk drive, printer, etc.), or with the network (a number of computers linked together). "Sometimes I'll go to a customer's business and check the site for a network installation. I have to consider the size and shape of the building, how many floors it has, things like that. I recommend where the computer terminals should be set up and where holes should be drilled in the walls to link them together. I also recommend the type of system that would best suit the customer's business needs.

"There are no set hours," says Rob. "Sometimes I have to work early or late. It really depends on what has to be done."

Getting the job

Rob was always interested in electronics. "I was caught tinkering with a soldering iron when I was four years old," laughs Rob. "When I was a little older, I would fix radios for friends and relatives. Later, I learned to fix computers just as I used to fix radios. My present employer knew me and was willing to hire me on a trial basis, to see how things would work out. I guess it was a lucky break."

Most of Rob's skills with computers were not learned in school. "I learned most of what I know on my own. But it's not easy to get your foot in the door. Even to get some interviews, a higher education would help."

Getting started

1. Read about computers and take computer courses in school.
2. Use computers in your spare time, and perhaps make them a hobby.
3. Take math in school to improve your thinking skills and problem-solving skills.
4. Find out as much as you can about all sorts of electronic devices — radios, televisions, and other gadgets — as well as computers.
5. Read magazines to keep up-to-date on what's happening in the computer industry.

Jan Shepherd — Artist and Curator

"I make it my business to find new ways to visualize things," says Jan Shepherd. "As an artist, I try to express what I think is important. I want to find new technologies and the people to help me use them, so I've begun to work with engineers."

Jan's career is divided between her work as a professional artist and her work as a curator. A curator is a person in charge of a collection at a gallery or museum. "I live in my studio," says Jan, "so when I get up in the morning I can start working." It's through her work as a curator that she has pursued her interest in technology.

Engineers and artists

Recently, Jan organized a public show called "Art and New Technologies" at an art gallery. Its purpose was to illustrate that art and science need not be separated. She feels that only in the modern age have people thought the two are separate. "This is a mistake," she says. "It's important to bring them together again. In this show, there were two groups of creative people: engineers who build practical things like bridges and roads, and artists who produce works such as paintings and sculptures. My job was to get things started and be in charge of the show. I got the people together and let things happen."

When Jan began this project, she had a clear purpose in mind. "I wanted people to know that technology is not something of the future; it is something we live with now. I also wanted to show that engineers can be creative and artists can be technical; the merging of the two occurs quite easily. And finally, I wanted artists and engineers to find new ways to approach their work."

In the show were many examples of successful cooperation between artists and engineers. "One artist used a computer to design a sculpture the size of a building. When you're building a sculpture this big, you can't have it falling down on people.

Computer graphics allow free rein to the imagination. This image was created entirely on a computer.

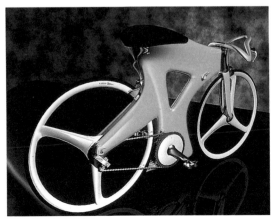

"I always wanted to be an artist, but I didn't tell anyone," Jan recalls. "I didn't think it was a respectable career, so I tried other things, including English literature and the philosophy of science."

You need to know about strengths and weaknesses of the materials and of the structure you are using. So I brought this artist together with some civil engineers and some materials engineers. They developed a work of art that was structurally sound."

Bringing science to non-scientists and bringing art to non-artists is important to Jan Shepherd. "I feel strongly that in the future there will be less specialization. We will need people who can be creative as they work. Being exposed to different disciplines is a way of opening your mind and becoming a more creative person."

Getting started

1. Do a lot of art. Draw, paint, take photographs, make videos, and try to use different media.
2. Learn to use a draw or paint program on a personal computer. There are lots of these programs available for just about any computer on the market.
3. Take a variety of subjects at school. Include math, science, visual arts, and literature.
4. Go to galleries and museums. You can see how others have approached their art in a wide variety of styles.
5. Become familiar with computers. Computers can create images unlike any that have been seen before.

Classified Advertising

HELP WANTED

COMPUTER OPERATIONS SUPERVISOR

Retail chain with P.O.S. (DOS), back office system (UNIX), accounting experience. Debra 444-4444

SENIOR Computer Artist needed as a Software Operator. Must have a minimum of 18 months' experience with similar software. 35 hr. work week, rotating shift work involved. Salary $36,400/yr. Please forward resumé to Box 2040, The Daily News, City, Province/State.

UNIX/C Programmer. Some international travel. Please call 647-2105.

LABORATORY Technician for time research position at local hospital. B.Sc. or M.Sc. experience in molecular biology required. Call 357-1492.

PHYSIOTHERAPIST

The Community Health Center is seeking a part-time therapist. This health center offers a multidisciplinary approach with special focus on Seniors, Education, and Health Promotion. Competitive salary and excellent benefits. Candidates must be eligible for registration with the Society of Physiotherapists.

Please send resumé by October 16, 19— Community Health Center 30 Smith St., Unit 201, City, Province/State; Attention: Executive Coordinator

Position Available

An inner-city Community Health Center, with community and clinical activities, is looking for experienced in the following positions:
Nurse Practitioner: B.Sc.N. or equivalent. Experience in community-based primary health care and program planning. Strong clinical skills required.
Health Promoter: Health promotion degree or equivalent. Demonstrated success in developing and implementing health promotion programs at a community level. Good communication and group facilitation skills required.
Community Health Worker: Social services degree or equivalent. Demonstrated success in developing and implementing community-based projects. Grassroots advocacy and community organizing experience an asset. Familiarity with community health issues and resources a must.
Successful candidates will have:
- experience with any of the following: street people, ex-psychiatric patients, low-income people, families in crisis, and/or immigrants.
- the ability to work well both independently, and as part of a multidisciplinary team.
- multicultural experience and/or knowledge of other languages

Send your reply, indicating the position you wish to apply for, to: Carol Klim, Program Coordinator, Central Community Health Center; 3 Augusta Avenue, City, Province/State; Fax 363-2115.

KEYBOARD DEPT. MANAGER

Responsible for inventory management, sales and marketing. Must be hardworking, with sales experience and product knowledge in some of the following: Home Keyboard, Pro Synthesis Home Recording, and Music Software. Sales Position available. Forward resumé to: **MusicComp, 392 Some St., City, Province/State**

Electronics Engineer

Traffic Systems Company Limited requires an Electronics Engineer successful...

...resume to:
...er of Mechanical Engineering Tech-op Ltd. 402 Maple St., City, Province/State (Tel. 7182; Fax ...

...thank all applicants for applying. However, only those under consideration will be contacted.

Manager, Environmental Services

Fuels, Inc. is seeking a bright, self-directed professional with a broad understanding of environmental issues to assist in the development and coordination of company environmental policies and programs.

...duties include participation in environmental assessments of new facility construction, review of operational procedures, waste management strategies, advising company departments and regions with respect to compliance with environmental legislation, environmental auditing, and maintaining... research and government... ...Inc.

The... ...minimum of 7 years... familiarity with... ...tributor. Strong... ...tive salary and... consideration,

...Inc.

...the distribution of ...security/fire/... systems. We are currently seeking individual to sell systems. This position will be based... our... office and will... approximately 20% field... Qualifications include a ...sales background in the electronic security/fire industry and strong interpersonal skills. For consideration and a local interview, applicants should forward resumés, complete with salary history, to: **Mr. R. Treed Security Inc. 319 Southfield Drive City, Province/State**

Pharmacist

You will be responsible for delivery of all inpatient, outpatient, and retail pharmacy services. This position requires a professional designation, and a minimum of 2 years' related experience within a retail or hospital pharmacy operation. Excellent communication skills and the ability to work independently are essential to your success in this job. The location will appeal to individuals who enjoy extensive outdoor recreation activities, including kayaking, boating, exploring many small islands, and fishing. Along with this wonderful, close-to-nature environment, the successful candidate will enjoy a competitive compensation package and a subsidized housing package. Qualified candidates are invited to apply to:

Administrator, R.W. Large Memorial Hospital City, Province/State, Postal Code/Zip Code; Tel: (000) 357-2314, Fax: (000) 357-2315

Who got the job?

Finding a job

The first step to success in any career is getting a job. But how do you go about finding one?

- Talk with family, friends, and neighbors and let them know what jobs interest you.

- Respond to "Help Wanted" ads in newspapers.

- Post an advertisement of your skills on a community bulletin board.

- Register at government employment offices or private employment agencies.
- Contact potential employers by phone or in person.

- Send out inquiry letters to companies and follow up with phone calls.

A job application usually consists of a letter and a resumé (a summary of your experience and qualifications for the job). Applicants whose resumés show they are qualified may be invited to a job interview.

Activity

A job in a games store

The advertisement shown on the opposite page, for an entry-level position in a store selling computer games, was placed in a local newspaper. Here is an opportunity for someone to turn a hobby into a paying job!

The ad directs applicants to go directly to the store, bringing a resumé. For a job like this, there might be many applicants, but only a few would later be granted interviews. Two of these applicants were Toni Anderson and David DePasquale. Their letters and resumés, and the notes made by Diane Thomas during the interviews, are shown on pages 46 and 47.

Procedure
Read the letters and the resumés and make notes about whether each applicant might qualify for the job. Use your notes and the interviewer's notes to list the strengths and weaknesses of each candidate. What else would you like to know about the applicants? How could each of them have improved on their letters, their resumés, or their performance during the interview? If you were Diane Thomas, which person would you hire: Toni or David?

Challenge
How would you perform in a job interview? Role-playing can give you practice in asking and answering questions. Have a friend take the part of Diane Thomas and interview you for this job. Then reverse roles. This practice can help ensure that when you apply for a job, you have a good chance of getting it!

David DePasquale's application and interview

14 Duke Street
Melonville, Province/State
Postal/Zip Code

October 12, 19—

Games Games Games
368 Industrial Road
Melonville, Province/State
Postal/Zip Code

Dear Manager:

I would like to apply for the position with your outlet as advertised in The Weekly News on October 10, 19—. I have included a resumé as requested.

I have worked part time for three years at Computer Universe in sales and service. I believe I have sufficient knowledge of all of the popular models of computers. I also have a basic understanding of electronics and computer circuitry.

I have good communications skills and a great deal of experience in customer relations.

Also, in my many years as a computer buff, I have seen many video games. I am familiar with how they work and which ones are most popular.

Please call me at 555-8762 to arrange an interview.

Sincerely,

David De Pasquale

David DePasquale

David's interview
- He demonstrated a wide knowledge of computers, talked a lot about bugs and bytes.
- He appeared to be interested in learning more—he asked questions about where he could find more information.
- He was interested in finding out what he should do if he couldn't handle a customer's difficult questions.
- While he was personable and enthusiastic, he was extremely casual, wore jeans and a T-shirt.

Resumé

David DePasquale
14 Duke Street
Melonville, Province/State
Postal/Zip Code
Telephone: 555-8762

Job Experience
Computer Universe, Sales and Service (part time). Deal with customers and co-workers. Handle inventories, minor repairs of hardware, and many odd jobs.

19— - 19—
Worked in a small butcher's shop as an assistant. Wrapped meat products, made sales, and kept site clean.

19— - 19—
Delivered local newspaper every day for six years. Made sure paper was delivered on time to every household.

Education
Graduation Diploma, Melonville High School

Strong subjects included math, computer science, and gym. Interests and activities included music (guitar); computers; soccer; and coaching six-year-olds in hockey.

References
Melissa Harwood
Owner, Computer Universe
35 Dale Avenue
Telephone: 555-2626

Alex Amin
2050 Ark Boulevard
Hillcrest, Province/State
Telephone: 555-7645

Toni Anderson's application and interview

2565 Allan Street
Melonville, Province/State
Postal/Zip Code

October 11, 19—

Games Games Games
368 Industrial Road
Melonville, Province/State
Postal/Zip Code

Dear Ms. Thomas:

It was with great interest that I read your ad in yesterday's The Weekly News.

I work part time at a video store that also rents video games. I am quite knowledgeable with regard to video games. I have been a fan of video games for years and am familiar with all types. I think I would be an enthusiastic addition to your team.

Thank you for taking the time to check my qualifications. My resumé is included for your consideration.

Sincerely yours,

Toni Anderson

Toni Anderson

Resumé

Toni Anderson
2565 Allan Street
Melonville, Province/State
Postal/Zip Code
Telephone: 555-7890

Education
19— - 19—

Melonville High School
24 Blue Valley Road
Melonville, Province/State
- Graduation Diploma
- courses in art, history, and computers
- school field hockey team

Work Experience
19— - Present

Video Station Plus
Melonville, Province/State
Work as salesclerk, stocking shelves, helping customers.

19— - 19—

Simone's Diner
Melonville, Province/State
Served customers in friendly and courteous manner.
Part-time employment.

References

Available on request

Toni's interview
• She talked about smart-bombs and invading aliens.
• She obviously loves games, but was not very knowledgeable about computers.
• She knew a lot about inventory systems, having learned about them at her previous job.
• She was appropriately dressed and spoke well. She had no questions about what her responsibilities would be.

Index

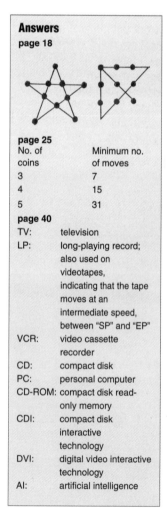

Answers
page 18

page 25

No. of coins	Minimum no. of moves
3	7
4	15
5	31

page 40

TV:	television
LP:	long-playing record; also used on videotapes, indicating that the tape moves at an intermediate speed, between "SP" and "EP"
VCR:	video cassette recorder
CD:	compact disk
PC:	personal computer
CD-ROM:	compact disk read-only memory
CDI:	compact disk interactive technology
DVI:	digital video interactive technology
AI:	artificial intelligence

Credits

(l = left; r = right; t = top; b = bottom; c = center; bl = bottom left; br = bottom right)

All art by Warren Clark, except 5 Lindquist Avey Macdonald Baskerville Inc.; 8 Lindquist Avey Macdonald Baskerville Inc.; 30(c) Max Beimler; 30(b) Matrix Design Consultants; 32 Patrick J. Winter; 43(b) Alias Research Inc.

All photographs by Catherine Rimmi, except 9 Metropolitan Toronto Police; 13(t) James D. Rising; 14 Archives of Ontario (AD 1475); 17 From *Math in Context 7*, by Ebos et al. Copyright 1992. Used by permission of Nelson Canada, a division of Thomson Canada Limited; 18 David Rising; 23 Chrysler Canada Ltd.; 24(b) Snowbird Software Inc., Hamilton Ont.; 29 Bell Canada Telephone Historical Collection; 31(t) Matrix Design Consultants; 32 David Rising; 33 Courtesy of the Royal Ontario Museum, Toronto, Ontario; 34 David Rising; 35 David Rising; 36 David Rising; 38(t) and (b) David Rising; 39 David Rising; 40(t) Michael Crichlow; 40(b) Bell Canada Telephone Historical Collection; 41(b) Thomas Foreign Exchange/Thomas Cook Currency Services Inc.; 42 Dave Mazzarolo; 43(t) Patrick Brennan.